THE RHS GARDEN WISLEY

In 1903, Sir Thomas Hanbury gave Wisley Garden in trust to the Royal Horticultural Society. His wish was that the Society 'use and occupy Wisley Estate or such portion thereof as the Society may require for the purpose of an Experimental Garden and the Encouragement and the Improvement of Scientific and Practical Horticulture in all its branches'. In almost a century of occupation the Society's aims and objectives for Wisley have remained true to Sir Thomas' wishes.

As a result the Garden is now a renowned showplace for all aspects of horticultural practice and a living catalogue of ornamental and culinary plants. The education of current and future generations of gardeners and horticulturists is regarded as a priority and is managed through a student gardener training course, a special programme for schools and a series of workshops and lectures for anyone interested in acquiring a greater level of expertise.

For all these reasons Wisley remains a major influence on our nation's gardening heritage.

ABOUT THE GUIDE

Our guide to the RHS Garden Wisley takes you on a tour of the garden, from the Laboratory, up the Broad Walk to Battleston Hill and ending finally at Howard's Field at the opposite end of the garden. We have introduced a circular route which visits every area of Wisley, but of course visitors are free to choose their own route and the map key (opposite) identifies each area of the garden. For ease of reference within the guide, the map key has been ordered to match the circular route described above.

The map has been colour coded to distinguish the six distinct areas of the garden around which the guide is based. Each map section is repeated at the start of each of the six areas as a quick reference, and continued in miniature on the relevant pages throughout that section.

We hope you enjoy your visit to Wisley and find this booklet a useful and informative guide to this important national garden.

The Royal Horticultural Society was given Wisley in 1903, although at that time only a small part of the 24-ha (60-acre) estate was actually cultivated as a garden, the remainder being wooded farmland. The original garden was the creation of George Ferguson Wilson – businessman, scientist, inventor and keen gardener and a former Treasurer of the Society. In 1878 he purchased the site and established the 'Oakwood experimental garden', with the idea of making 'difficult plants grow successfully'. The garden acquired a reputation for its collections of lilies, gentians, Japanese irises, primulas and water plants. The present Wild Garden (p.38) is the direct descendant of Oakwood and despite changes is still true to the original concept.

After Wilson's death in 1902, Oakwood and the adjoining Glebe Farm were bought by Sir Thomas Hanbury, a wealthy Quaker who had founded the celebrated garden of La Mortola, on the Italian Riviera. In 1903, Sir Thomas presented the Wisley estate in trust to the Society for its perpetual use.

Nothing could have been more providential in the circumstances. For at least 30 years, the Society had been seeking a larger garden 'beyond the radius of the London smoke', to replace the garden at Chiswick which it had leased since 1822. It was also committed to building a new exhibition hall and offices in Vincent Square (and the construction work had

A late winter view from the top of the Rock Garden looking towards the Wild Garden and Seven Acres

Plant trials are an important part of the Society's work. Here the dahlia trial is ready for assessment in late summer

WISLEY

Autumn spectacular in Seven Acres as the foliage of *Liquidambar styraciflua* takes on its fiery tints

Visitors enjoying the blaze of colour from the rhododendrons in flower on Battleston Hill in the late spring sunshine

already started). Both projects were seen as a fitting way to celebrate the Society's forthcoming centenary in 1904 but there were heated arguments among the Fellows over which should have priority for the available funds. Sir Thomas' generous donation solved both these problems at a stroke. By May 1904, the move from Chiswick to Wisley was complete and, in July, the new headquarters at Vincent Square was officially opened by King Edward VII – both in time to mark the centenary.

While Wisley was taking shape as an ornamental garden, its educational and scientific roles were never forgotten. A small laboratory was opened and the School of Horticulture founded to instruct young people in the principles of horticulture and prepare them for careers as professional gardeners. Many leading horticulturists have benefited from the School of Horticulture including Robert Fortune, one of the great plant hunters and Joseph Paxton who was later knighted for designing the Crystal Palace.

Following the move to Wisley the trials of flowers, vegetables and fruit – an important part of the Society's work since 1860 – were resumed and expanded. The trials 'epitomise...the Society's endeavour to show to the public the best kinds of plants to grow' and remain one of the principal objects of the Garden. That combination of learning with pleasure is the essence of Wisley.

THE SITE

Over 6,000 people visited Wisley during its first year under the Society's control and those who criticised its inaccessible position were quickly silenced by 'the great development of road traction'. Others considered the situation and soil most unsuitable. The latter is naturally acid sand, which is poor in nutrients and fast draining, although in places well supplied with water. Lying in the valley of the River Wey, the Garden is vulnerable to frequent harsh frosts, often continuing into May and early June, and it is also exposed to biting north-east winds. Wisley has been hit by freak weather on several occasions – both severe flooding and devastating winds, even a tornado, which have left a trail of destruction in their wake. Growing conditions at Wisley are certainly not easy, but in this respect it is an ideal testing

Above: the entrance to the Garden has changed greatly from this, the original entrance to G F Wilson's Oakwood

Right: one of Wisley's primary aims is to educate and a School of Horticulture was founded in 1907 for the training of student gardeners. The original classrooms were remodelled when the new Laboratory was built but the lecture theatre has remained an important part of the building

Right: the new tudor-style Laboratory photographed around 1915-16 as the building neared completion

ground for plants: if they succeed here, they will (except for lime-hating plants) have a good chance of succeeding almost anywhere in Britain.

A garden of this size has always relied upon the commitment and energy of its staff to ensure that the garden fulfills its role of inspiring and educating its visitors. There are currently 79 garden staff including students, 59 members of the Science and Education departments and 26 Administration staff. For many, Wisley becomes a life's work and former students return to become valued staff members.

Today the Garden occupies approximately 97ha (240 acres) and the number of visitors each year is approaching 750,000. Like any garden, Wisley is a dynamic place: the devastating storms of 1987 and 1990 acted as a facelift, speeding up the pace of change and giving scope to rethink and redevelop major areas.

Above: photographed shortly after completion in 1916, the Laboratory stands proudly at the entrance to the Garden. Built from recycled materials from old manor houses, it gives the impression of a grand country house much older than it is in reality

ENTRANCE AREA

ENTRANCE

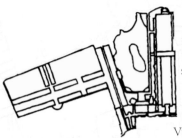

On entering the Garden, immediately ahead on your right is a massive 220-year-old oak tree whose branches have naturally grafted themselves together, often a sign of pollarding in the past – look for the resulting circled or looped branches. Just beside it is the little gatehouse where, until 1962, everyone was requested to sign the Visitors' Book.

To enter the Garden go through the imposing wrought-iron gates. These are emblazoned with the date of the Society's founding in 1804 and commemorate the Rev. William Wilks. To him we owe the well-known Shirley poppies – also part of the gate design.

LABORATORY AND CANAL

Passing through the gates, to your right is the focal point of the Garden, the half-timbered building known as the Laboratory. It looks older than it is, in part because it was built during 1914-16 of materials recycled from old manor houses around the district. The mellow brick walls, south and west facing, support many slightly tender or early flowering climbers and shrubs.

Although it has the appearance of a comfortable home, the Laboratory was purpose built to house a lecture theatre and classrooms for the School of Horticulture. It now accommodates the administration and scientific departments.

This magnificent building overlooks a formal

CLIMBERS AND SHRUBS

Actinidia kolomikta
Azara serrata
Callistemon rigidus
Camellia japonica
  'Princess Charlotte'
Carpenteria californica 'Bodnant'
Feijoa sellowiana
Grevillea rosmarinifolia
Parthenocissus henryana
Rosa 'Climbing Lady Hillingdon'
Rosa gigantea
Viburnum foetens
Vitex agnus-castus

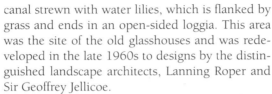

canal strewn with water lilies, which is flanked by grass and ends in an open-sided loggia. This area was the site of the old glasshouses and was redeveloped in the late 1960s to designs by the distinguished landscape architects, Lanning Roper and Sir Geoffrey Jellicoe.

Along one side is a broad mixed border facing south backed by shrubs with perennials and half-hardy plants designed for summer impact. On the other side, a recent development is the long series of raised beds and the planting on the bank which has opened up views of the Conifer Lawn.

Walk the length of the canal with the Conifer Lawn on your left to the loggia and into the Formal and Walled Gardens.

Above left: the severe winter of 1962/63
Above: Mr Holloway, the Gate Attendant and custodian of the visitors' book, at the door of his 'lodge' below the pollarded oak, about 1947

Below: View from the front of the Laboratory. The open-sided loggia at the end of the canal was once the potting shed. It has been constructed to give the impression of being a bridge

Above: the square of carpet bedding in front of the Laboratory is planted each year to a different design. This teaches student gardeners the techniques required for this intricate form of bedding

Below: The original glasshouse range was situated where the long canal is now

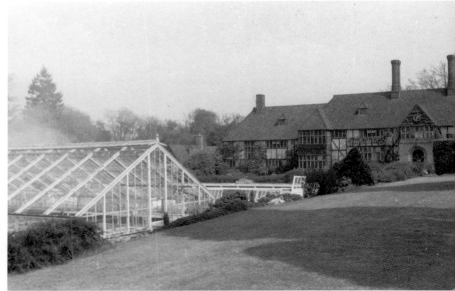

FORMAL GARDEN

Beyond the loggia lies the Formal Garden and the Walled Garden, bisected by a path lined with clipped yew hedges.

The first is laid out as a formal parterre and used for a variety of spring and summer bedding schemes, creating a rainbow of colour visible from the Laboratory building.

Left: with its spectacular planting of flowers, foliage and trailing plants, the urn is the centrepiece of the Formal Garden. Frequent attention is needed to maintain a planting like this

Below: the planting in the Formal Garden is changed with the seasons and the resulting bedding schemes are carefully planned to provide a contrast of colour and form

WALLED GARDEN

An archway draped with roses leads to the second more intimate walled garden which was redeveloped in 2000 with generous sponsorship from Witan Investments. This walled enclosure has proved an ideal microclimate for demonstrating warm temperate gardening in a cold climate with mixed plantings of hardy and tender plants. The different aspects of the walls allow a range of climbing plants to thrive and at each end of the garden two cascades recycle water from the central water feature via rills. With the sound of water and the scent of nearby plants, this is a perfect retreat on a hot summer day.

The double gates at the far end commemorate Ken Aslet, a Wisley staff member from 1949–75 and for many years Superintendent of the Rock Garden. Other gates are dedicated to Frank Knight, Director of Wisley from 1955–69 and W D Cartwright, who worked at Wisley for 44 years.

Exit via the gate between the hedges that separates these two gardens to face the Conifer Lawn. The south-facing exterior of the wall provides a sheltered, sunny site for climbers such *Wisteria*. This aspect is also important for the hot border immediately in front. Here *Iris unguicularis*, tender perennials, such as gazanias, and sub-shrubs bask happily in the hot sun.

Left: to one side of the Walled Garden is a south-facing border which offers an ideal position for growing tender perennials and sub-shrubs. A statue of Pan at the end of the border is embraced by the flowers of *Wisteria floribunda* 'Kuchi-Beni' and makes an appropriate focal point

CONIFER LAWN

Remnants of a small pinetum can be found on the slope opposite you. This early area of the Garden, where many more conifers once stood, boasts a Chilean incense cedar, *Austrocedrus chilensis,* a rare *Juniperus monosperma* with feathery foliage and, in 2000, a Henry Moore statue.

MIXED BORDERS

Cross the Conifer Lawn diagonally to the left to come to the Terrace, a wide path between lawns dotted with circular and oblong beds of seasonal bedding plants. From here enter the Mixed Borders, which are chief among the glories of Wisley. Each some 128m long by 6m wide (420 by 18ft), they rise gently towards Battleston Hill backed by hornbeam hedges.

The borders provide the visitor with a spectacle rich in plants, with shrubs to provide a framework and bulbs for interplanting. Composition is paramount, achieved through graded colour schemes and variations in textures and height. *Continue up the hill to Battleston Hill (p.14) or turn right halfway along into the Autumn Borders.*

Autumn Borders Running at right angles to the Mixed Borders are two smaller borders designed for late summer and autumn colour.

Below: the Mixed Borders were at one time the site of the dahlia trials

Right: looking down on the Conifer Lawn over the Canal towards the restaurant and cafe. The trees here are a remnant of a small pinetum and include some rare specimens

Left and opposite: one of the great glories of Wisley, the Mixed Borders provide exciting ideas for planting combinations and are at their most effective in July and August. The view on the left was taken soon after sunrise

Above: the autumn borders, planted at right angles to the Mixed Borders, continue to provide interesting planting associations into September and October. The Bowes Lyon Memorial Pavilion is at the end of this vista

COUNTRY GARDEN

To the right (north) again of the Autumn Borders, at the foot of Weather Hill (p.30), a new garden is under construction to a design by Mrs Penelope Hobhouse. Her brief was to create a cottage style garden using a mixture of small trees, shrubs, perennials and bulbs in an arrangement which might be appropriate to any smaller garden. The garden has been planned to include a natural style of planting inside a fairly tight structure created by the use of small trees, background hedges and pathways. Each area within the overall scheme could be an entire garden while at the same time it is linked to the others to form a whole.

The garden was completed and officially opened in July 2000.

GARDEN FOR NEW ROSE INTRODUCTIONS

The garden for new rose introductions lies above (to the west of) the new Country Garden, separated by the Autumn Borders. Over 200 cultivars of bush and pillar rose introduced during the previous 10 years are on view and the garden is topped up annually with introductions from the current year. Once past the 10-year limit, the roses are either planted elsewhere at Wisley or discarded. Each year a section of soil is sterilized to prevent it becoming 'rose sick' before the latest additions are planted.

Turn left at the top of this garden, along the paved road, to rejoin the Broad Walk at the base of Battleston Hill above the Mixed Borders.

Right: the Garden for New Rose Introductions is planted as an exhibition of roses introduced into cultivation over the last 10 years

COUNTRY GARDEN PLANTS OF INTEREST

Hydrangea paniculata 'Kyushu'
Iris ensata
Malus sieboldii 'Professor Sprenger'
Philadelphus 'Innocence'
Phlox paniculata 'Fujiyama'
Stipa gigantea
Zantedeschia aethiopica

Above: alliums are surrounded by French lavender (*Lavandula stoechas*) in one of the purple borders in the Country Garden

Left and far left: the view through the centre of the Country Garden, where water flowing gently over a flat, circular, stone fountain (left), is framed by metal arches (far left). The white stone sculpture is part of a changing display throughout Wisley

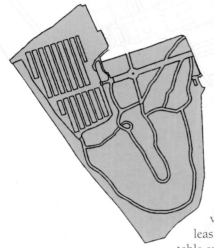

The Broad Walk, the path between the long Mixed Borders leads to the foot of Battleston Hill, a high wooded ridge running from east to west and falling away on the far side to the Portsmouth Field. A visit to this part in May and June, when it is vibrant with the vivid colours of azaleas and rhododendrons, is an unforgettable experience.

BATTLESTON HILL AND BATTLESTON EAST

Battleston Hill has been transformed since the storms of 1987 and 1990 which did so much damage to the woodland and mature trees that formed a major part of this area. Battleston East experienced most change and is now much more accessible with solid or wood chipped paths. The shelter belts which formed Battleston Hill's initial plantings are gradually being thinned so as to allow those remaining to become specimen trees.

Hardy hybrid rhododendrons grow to the left of the Broad Walk up the hill. This is a showcase for many excellent cultivars which have received

Above: early planting on Battleston Hill. This area underwent major reconstruction following the storms of 1987 and 1990

Right: the fall of a giant – the root plate of a cedar tree. This was one of many casualties of storm damage in 1990

awards from the Society. Further up are three beds of smaller rhododendron hybrids, in particular the progeny of *R. yakushimanum*. Low-growing, compact, hardy and floriferous, they have everything to recommend them for the smaller garden.

To the right of the main walk are evergreen hybrid azaleas. Prominent among them are the Kurume azaleas, introduced in 1918 from a Japanese nursery by the famous plant collector, E H Wilson, and considered by him to be 'the loveliest of all Azaleas'.

Although rhododendrons are the stars of Battleston Hill, there are many other fine plants to enjoy throughout the seasons. In January and February, *Hamamelis* and *Sarcococca* fill the air with their fragrance and March and April bring displays of camellias and magnolias.

Herbaceous plants provide additional interest during the summer, ranging from primulas and hostas through the large collection of lilies to *Agapanthus* and even the moisture-loving *Gunnera* and *Darmera*.

A new sculpture on the brow of the hill is a focal point for the entire length of the broad walk. The sculpture, entitled 'Naissance' is the work of Donald Foxley and has been purchased following the generous donations of RHS members and visitors to the Garden. From this vantage point it is possible to view large parts of the Garden and surrounding countryside.

Left: the majestic beauty of the Scots pine dominates Battleston East. The area is doubly worth visiting in spring to see the collection of magnolias in flower

Left: in late spring and early summer the rhododendrons provide a gloriously vibrant patchwork of colour throughout this area. Shown here is a group of deciduous azaleas with particularly handsome flowers

Below: at the bottom of Battleston Hill the season of interest extends into summer with the large collection of herbaceous perennials and flowering shrubs This group includes *Hemerocallis*, *Agapanthus* and *Hydrangea paniculata*

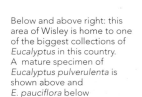

MEDITERRANEAN GARDEN

In the hottest part of the Garden, on the slope down from the top of the Broad Walk to the Portsmouth Field below, a feature has been developed which can be loosely described as the Mediterranean Garden. The site was part of the area devastated by the 1987 storm which ripped away much of the tree cover. The steepest part of the resulting dry, south-facing slope has been terraced with railway sleepers.

This area contains many sun-loving plants from the Mediterranean, Australasia, California and some hardy South African plants.

Below and above right: this area of Wisley is home to one of the biggest collections of *Eucalyptus* in this country. A mature specimen of *Eucalyptus pulverulenta* is shown above and *E. pauciflora* below

16

Included in the planting scheme are *Ceanothus*, *Cistus*, *Salvia* and *Eucalyptus*, as well as herbaceous plants and bulbs for different seasons.

The strip of woodland at the southern end of the Portsmouth Field has been planted for interest between November and March. There are winter-flowering and berrying plants, and those with bark interest such as *Acer grosseri* var. *hersii*.

MEDITERRANEAN GARDEN PLANTS OF INTEREST

Abutilon x *suntense*
Ceanothus
Eucalyptus (one of the finest collections in the country)
Euphorbia mellifera
Genista aetnensis
Olearia phlogopappa 'Comber's Blue'
Phlomis fruticosa
Pittosporum tobira
Yucca flaccida 'Ivory'

Below: the fascinating striped bark of *Acer grosseri* var. *hersii* makes this tree one of winter's highlights

Left: the plants which thrive in this hot dry area of the garden mostly originate in regions with a Mediterranean-type climate. This area was developed after the storm of 1987 destroyed the tree cover

Below: a welcome sight in early spring, the fragrant, delicate-looking flowers of camellias brighten any area. The cultivars of *Camellia* x *williamsii* are among the best for general planting

PORTSMOUTH FIELD

This gently sloping area is the main trials area of the Society where plants are grown specifically for the purpose of comparing the different cultivars available and assessing their merits. Trials are of two types – long standing and invited. Long-standing trials, which continue from year to year, include dahlias, delphiniums, chrysanthemums and sweet peas.

Invited trials of selected crops, which change each year, concentrate on annual and biennial flowers, plus some perennials, and vegetables, and also pot plants in the Glasshouses. These trials are open to everyone – amateur gardeners and professional seedsmen – who are 'invited' to submit seeds or plants from the calendar of trials which appears in the RHS journal, *The Garden,* each autumn.

Trials entries raised from seed are normally grown under number and cultivar name, and a

Above: the annual trials may change but the layout of Portsmouth Field has changed little from this early photograph taken around the 1950s

Below and right: at any time of year there are trials of interest in the Portsmouth Field but perhaps some of the most spectacular are to be seen in the summer. Sweetpeas (right) and delphiniums (below) are both long-standing trials. It is an excellent opportunity for the visitor to compare the qualities and characteristics of many different cultivars

detailed record of their growth is kept by the Trials Department. Information boards, detailing entries, cultivation processes and award recommendations, are displayed adjacent to each trial.

All plants are inspected by the appropriate committees of the Society, who can often be observed carrying out their duties. Based on their recommendations the prestigious Award of Garden Merit may be given. The trials are one of the most important aspects of the work of the Garden.

Also found on the trials field is the National Collection of Rhubarb. This is one of the oldest collections having been transferred to Wisley in 1904 from the Society's earlier Chiswick Garden. The collection now includes 93 cultivars.

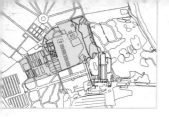

glassed-in corridor outside the Singapore Orchid House there is a collection of cacti donated to the Society by Sir Peter Smithers from his collection at Vico Morcote in Switzerland. These plants were selected by him for their flowering display.

THE VINERY
Two further glasshouses accessible from the Main Display House are used for the trials and seasonal displays. At the far end of one of these lies the Vinery. This accommodates a range of grape cultivars suitable for growing under glass.

Below: grape vines are carefully trained around the walls and roof of the vinery to allow maximum light and air to all parts of the vines

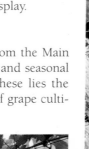

THE SUB-TROPICAL BORDER
As winters at Wisley have become less harsh, the Sub-tropical Border has left the shelter of the glasshouses and can now be found between the Model Herb Garden and the Garden of the Senses (see p.30) leading to Weather Hill. Twin 30m borders luxuriate in sub-tropical plantings of cannas, bananas (*Musa* species) and *Melianthus*.

Above: autumn's show stoppers – the charm and cascade chrysanthemums – are old favourites of Wisley visitors and are displayed every year in the cool section of the Main Display House

Opposite: banana palms emerge from the Glasshouses every summer to provide an exotic elegance to the Sub-tropical Border

Right: A statue of Eros is the focal point in an area which comprises an interesting mix of stone, gravel and plants in the *Evening Standard*'s Eros Garden

Opposite: the Agriframes Living Rooms Garden demonstrates the ornamental value of various climbers grown over a selection of arches and pillars. One of the interesting features of the garden is this appealing bust

Located between the Glasshouses and the rose borders of Weather Hill (p.30), the Model Gardens have been created specifically with the needs of the average home garden in mind and offer a selection of practical ideas. Walking from the Glasshouses through the model garden area the visitor encounters the gardens in the following order moving down the right hand side of the path and returning up the left hand side.

EROS (1)

The *Evening Standard* Eros Garden, a medal winner at the 1995 Chelsea Flower Show, was installed at Wisley in 1996. It illustrates just what can be achieved in a small courtyard garden. Look for the woven willow hedge surrounding the garden and the trained whitebeam (*Sorbus aria*) trees forming the gazebo and gate arch.

CONTAINER GARDEN (2)

This is an exciting display of patio pots and containers. Some are planted with trees, shrubs and other perennials, while others change with the seasons and brim with bedding plants. At the rear a gazebo supports hanging baskets.

GARDEN FOR NATURE (3)

The small wildlife garden situated to the rear of the Container Garden was also featured at the 1995 Chelsea Flower Show. Designed by Hilde Wainstein and sponsored by Camas Building Materials with support from the RSPB, the garden relies on British native plants.

LIVING ROOMS GARDEN (4)

The Agriframes Living Rooms Garden, designed by Ann Kennedy, contains a diverse collection of

1. Eros
2. Container Garden
3. Garden for Nature
4. Living Rooms Garden
5. *The Daily Telegraph* Reflective Garden
6. Town Garden
7. Family Garden
8. Enthusiast's Garden
9. Garden of the Senses
10. Model Herb Garden
11. Model Fruit Garden

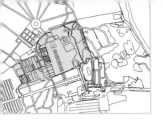

climbers and wall plants grown over arches and pergolas. It shows how a garden can be divided by vertical supports and interlinking water features.

THE DAILY TELEGRAPH REFLECTIVE GARDEN (5)

Originally awarded Best Garden in Show at the 1999 Chelsea Flower Show, this Gold-medal winning garden has been rebuilt at Wisley to extend the range of the Model Gardens into the 21st century. Exploiting the beauty of modern tensile fabrics supported by gleaming steel masts, it deliberately contrasts modern sculptural forms with traditional planting. At its focus is a curved stainless steel wall that stands out brilliantly against the rich textural planting.

TOWN GARDEN (6)

A new garden for this site will be developed during the year 2000.

FAMILY GARDEN (7)

This slightly larger garden, sponsored by Rolawn, recognizes the demands of family life, with a patio, barbecue, children's play area, utility area and quiet sitting places.

ENTHUSIAST'S GARDEN (8)

Sponsored by Sainsbury's Homebase and designed by Robin Williams, this garden pays attention to design and planting associations using a wide and varied range of plants. Completed in spring 1997 within a year it had already become a well-established and popular garden.

GARDEN OF THE SENSES (9)

A continuing display of year round bonsai trees is supplemented by seasonal displays of Japanese maples and Satsuki azaleas generously donated by Herons Bonsai. These artfully trained trees complement the rock and gravel surfaces which provide variations in texture.

MODEL HERB GARDEN (10)

Formally arranged with box hedges, urns and a sundial in the centre, the Herb Garden contains a wide assortment of culinary and medicinal herbs, mixed with aromatic plants. Tea and tisane plants, insect-repelling plants and economic plants are given special sections.

Below: living up to the name, the tensile fabric sails and steel masts are clearly reflected in the stepped canal of *The Daily Telegraph Reflective Garden*

MODEL FRUIT GARDEN (11)

There are many lessons demonstrated in the Model Fruit Garden on how to obtain a good yield of hardy fruits from a small garden. Modern dwarfing rootstocks are used for apples and pears, and trees are trained as spindlebushes and in restricted forms as cordons, espaliers, fans and pyramids. Soft fruits – black, white and red currants, gooseberries and raspberries – are grown too, some as standards, but strawberries have been allocated a separate plot, where a system of soil rotation can be practised.

The westerly section contains a large collection of soft fruits and some examples of less familiar fruits, such as blueberries and jostaberries, as well as grapes, apricots and peaches. The latter are protected with a polythene screen in winter against peach leaf curl.

Above: the Model Herb Garden is based on a formal design in which the beds are used to grow the various categories of herbs

Left: the Model Fruit Garden displays a range of fruit that can be grown in containers outside and under glass

Right: a plaque commemorating the late Sir David Bowes Lyon, President of the Society from 1953-61, is dropped into position in the Bowes Lyon Memorial Pavilion on Weather Hill in 1964

Between the Model Herb Garden and Garden of the Senses, two broad sub-tropical borders flank the grass path leading to Weather Hill. Formerly situated by the glasshouses, each exotic 30m (98½ft) border is packed with tender and hardy plants (see p.24).

unusual and distinctive specimen trees such as the fossil tree, *Ginkgo biloba*. This area was recently supplemented by a collection of trees for the smaller garden that will provide bark, flower, fruit and leaf interest through the year.

WEATHER HILL

This area takes its name from the meteorological station which once stood at the top, before being moved to the Fruit Field. It is home to many

ROSE BORDERS AND CATENARY

The roses in the two long borders on the southern side of Weather Hill are graded according to

Below: Hannah Gordon, a fine, weather-resistant cluster-flowered rose cultivar

Right: a collection of climbing and rambler roses is trained over the catenary of oak posts linked by ropes that stretches down the length of both the rose borders on Weather Hill. 'Rambling Rector' is one of the vigorous ramblers used for this purpose

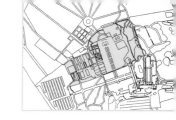

colour, planted upwards darker to lighter from the bottom. Large-flowered and cluster-flowered bush roses, better known as hybrid teas and floribundas, are still the most popular roses in English gardens and Weather Hill is the place to see them growing in splendid isolation. On its southern side a new magnolia and rose border has been planted. The roses have been selected for their disease resistance and longevity of flowering. On the far side of each of the rose borders the reinstated rose catenary of oak posts and ropes support twin chains of a variety of climbing roses.

BOWES LYON MEMORIAL PAVILION

This hilltop focal point was completed in 1964 to commemorate Sir David Bowes Lyon, President of the Society from 1953 to 1961, and brother of HM Queen Elizabeth the Queen Mother (herself a patron of the Society). The simple teak canopy of linked octagonal roofs on slender posts was designed according to a system of geometric proportion reflecting the columnar theme of an area dominated by two magnificent specimens of *Fagus sylvatica* 'Dawyck' on either side of the pavilion.

Above: a heavy early January frost transforms Weather Hill into a glittering icy spectacle that is as beautiful as when it is in full flower

THE ALPINE HOUSES

To the north of the Bowes Lyon Memorial Pavilion lie the Alpine Houses. The original house of 1926 was replaced by two houses, the Alpine Display House and the Landscape Alpine House, in 1984. The area around the houses faces north and is divided into three levels by drystone walls, constructed of different materials – Purbeck stone at the top and middle, Sussex sandstone at the bottom. The crevices in the walls accommodate a fascinating variety of plants from lewisias and zauschnerias higher up to shade-loving *Ramonda myconi* in the lowest spots.

ALPINE DISPLAY HOUSE

This traditional wooden alpine display house on the top terrace is used for displaying alpines and bulbous plants grown in pots. These are plunged into sand on the benches to keep watering to a minimum and are changed regularly to reflect the range of alpines in flower. New or reintroduced species collected from mountains all over the world are represented, together with early-flowering plants which can be grown to perfection when sheltered from winter weather.

Part of the National Collection of *Crocus* may be viewed in the Alpine Display House. Wisley is the custodian of 115 species and 68 cultivars of crocus which flower in winter, spring or autumn. Many are also found planted outdoors around the garden and *C. tommasinianus* provides much of the colour in the Alpine Meadow (p.36) in spring.

To grow many of these plants to perfection, the Roy Elliott Alpine Supply House was donated to the Society in 1991 by the Alpine Garden Society and the family of the late Roy Elliott, an alpine enthusiast who served on RHS Council.

Against the display house is a south-facing rock bank of tufa, a very porous limestone, in which many fascinating plants flourish. Between this house and Weather Hill are two raised beds, one housing lime-tolerant plants, the other lime haters.

LANDSCAPE ALPINE HOUSE

This house was rebuilt during 1995-96 with generous financial assistance from the East Surrey Group of the Alpine Garden Society, Hendry Bequest Fund. A simulated dry gully runs between miniature cliffs up to 1.5m (5ft) high. The cliffs demonstrate several rock types and provide niches for difficult-to-please alpines. The irrigation system is hidden beneath broken stones

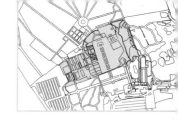

and the very gritty soil behind the rockwork. It is computer controlled with irrigation lines terminating in over 100 bubble points which trickle water gently to the root systems. Two large fans circulate air, assisted by louvred vents along the side walls and large ridge vents running the length of the house. Outside, the theme continues, demonstrating various rock types and aspects and the alpines that grow well in these situations.

HYPERTUFA SINKS AND STONE TROUGHS

On the lower terrace, these sinks and troughs are ideal for small slow-growing alpines which nestle between pieces of rock and slate and maintain a succession of bloom throughout the year. More vigorous plants fill the gaps in the paving, which is a creamy buff colour to heighten the impression of light.

Below: the remodelled . Landscape Alpine House nearing completion in 1996 The white plastic pipes visible between the rocks form the drainage system necessary to provide the sharply drained habitat preferred by most alpine plants. The rocks are positioned to simulate miniature cliffs

Left: spring bulbs bloom in the Alpine Display House. The plants are regularly changed to provide colour through the year

MONOCOT BORDERS

Two parallel beds border the pathway between the Alpine Houses and the Model Vegetable Garden. Backed by yew hedges, the monocot borders concentrate on one of the two great classes of flowering plants – the monocotyledons. These plants all share the same characteristics of having only one seed leaf, parallel leaf venation and flowers with three or multiples of three petals. The majority of the plants in these borders, such as *Crocosmia*, grasses and *Kniphofia*, are at their best in late summer and autumn.

Below: a study in contrasts: the brilliant yellow *Kniphofia* planted among scarlet *Crocosmia* 'Lucifer'

Right: the architectural impact of monocotyledons on planting schemes is admirably demonstrated here where a gigantic phormium dominates an array of *Kniphofia, Hemerocallis* and *Crocosmia*

MONOCOT BORDERS PLANTS OF INTEREST

Allium campanulatum
Allium cristophii
Camassia leichtlinii 'Electra'
Crocosmia x *crocosmiiflora* 'His Majesty'
Crocosmia 'Lucifer'
Hemerocallis 'Burning Daylight'
Iris sibirica 'Cambridge'
Kniphofia 'Red Admiral'
Tradescantia x *andersoniana* 'Zwanenberg Blue'
Yucca gloriosa

Right: *Hosta fortunei* var. *albopicta* and lilies make an interesting association

Left: the woodland habitat of the Wild Garden is ideal for hellebores such as this *Helleborus* x *sternii*

The soil in the Wild Garden is peaty and more moisture-retentive than elsewhere at Wisley, and was ideal for growing woodland plants until storms depleted the tree canopy. The long term objective is to restock the area with hostas, primulas, trilliums and the many other woodlanders that find the high water table and fertile soil so conducive to their growth. In 1990 a bamboo walk was introduced on the exposed south-west flank to filter the wind and this has become a great favourite with young visitors who can walk through the stands of bamboos over 10ft or more high. Over 30 different species and cultivars of bamboo may now be found in the Wild Garden.

Left: the Wild Garden is home to a wide variety of plant life with ferns growing along the banks of the stream while rhododendrons provide spring colour in the background

Below: the unusual colour combination of yellow and pink is provided by the flower spikes of *Ligularia przewalskii* and *Persicaria bistorta* 'Superba'. These plants enjoy the moist conditions found under the trees

Above: early morning mists surrounding the Lake create an eerie, magical atmosphere

SEVEN ACRES

Bounded by the Wild Garden, the River Wey, the Pinetum and the Restaurant, Seven Acres is an oblong piece of land of approximately that size (2.5ha). Originally rough pasture, it was regarded as useless for cultivation until, in the 1920s, an iron pan was discovered just below the surface and broken up so that plant roots could reach the water. This operation has allowed successful cultivation of plants ever since despite the sandy soil.

At the bottom of Seven Acres, attached to the Restaurant, is a long two-storey building – Aberconway House. Built in 1954 to mark 150 years of the Society and named for the 2nd Lord Aberconway, President of the RHS 1931-53, it is home to Wisley's students during their one or two year course. Two ground floor rooms are now home to the Library Reading Room, providing access to reference books and CD Roms for those unable to visit the Lindley Library in London.

To improve access around Seven Acres and encourage visitors to quieter parts of the garden, permanent pathways have recently been installed.

LAKE

At the Wild Garden end of Seven Acres, facing the Restaurant, the Lake is ahead on the left. This man-made pool is a major water feature here where the conical outlines of three dawn redwoods, *Metasequoia glyptostroboides*, are reflected in its waters above a fringe of *Gunnera* and several small willows. The Lake has a mood for each

Below: on a clear day a mirror image of the surrounding landscape and trees is visible in the water of the Lake

Right: this dramatic grass border is an inspiration for anyone yet to be won over by the attractions of grasses

season, particularly in summer when the water lilies are in flower and again in autumn when the redwoods are burnished pink and old gold.

ROUND POND

The Pond started life in Wisley's early developments as a source of gravel for garden paths and has remained as a water feature, shunning the adverse effects of drought every since. It sits to the east (right) of the lake but is often easy to miss because of the foliage surrounding it. On a little island (all that remains of a causeway that formerly spanned the pond) stands a deep green Japanese umbrella pine, *Sciadopitys verticillata*.

Over the next few years, the Lake and Round Pond will be dredged, the banks regraded and the plantings changed. Emphasis will be placed on the richness of the shrub collections together with herbaceous plantings of monocots such as *Hemerocallis, Kniphophia* and grasses.

GRASS BORDER

At the present time, leading from the pond along the edge of Seven Acres to the Restaurant is a dramatic grass border. At its best when in flower in late summer and autumn, many of the grasses in this border grow over 2.2 or 2.5m (7 or 8ft) high and provide an excellent example of group planting on a large scale. Over the next few years, however, as part of the development of Seven Acres, it is planned to integrate the grasses throughout this area rather than confining them to one border.

Below: *Nyssa sylvatica* 'Wisley Bonfire' and *Liquidambar styraciflua* are two of Seven Acres' spectacular autumn highlights

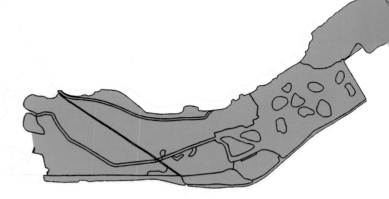

Above: in the early days a row of lilac trees ran the length of Howard's Field

Right: now home to the National Collection of heathers, spring in Howard's Field ushers in a blend of pinks in heather flowers and cherry blossom (here *Prunus serrula*)

CHAMPION TREES

The following trees are the tallest of their species found in Britain
Chamaecyparis lawsoniana 'Fletcheri'
Pinus bungeana
Pinus x holfordiana
Pinus ponderosa subsp. *scopulorum*
Pseudotsuga menziesii 'Fretsii'

There are two entrances and exits to the Pinetum from Seven Acres. Follow the path beside the pumping station, north-west of the Restaurant by the River Wey, which will take you under the ancient Public Right of Way which cuts through the Pinetum. This is the only way by which visitors in wheelchairs may enter or exit the Pinetum as the other is via a stepped bridge which goes over the Public Right of Way.

PINETUM

As elsewhere in the Garden, out of the upheaval created by storms has come the opportunity for major redevelopment in the Pinetum. Shrubs and trees chosen for autumn and spring colour, such as Japanese maples, witch hazels and flowering dogwoods, are being integrated with the existing conifers.

A stroll through the area of the Pinetum nearest to Seven Acres and the Restaurant will take the visitor among many fine old specimens from the collection of conifers and in early spring this area is also highlighted by naturalized narcissus.

Stroll through the Pinetum to Howard's Field or, depending on where you start, take the Riverside Walk along the River Wey.

HOWARD'S FIELD

The National Collection of heathers was relocated to Howard's Field in 1988/89. An irrigation system, with quantities of manure and leafmould dug in during the early stages of development, helps with the cultivation of these acid-loving plants in an area of otherwise pure sand. The heather beds, divided by meandering paths, have been placed for visual impact in groups of about 30 plants per cultivar. There are over 1,000 species and cultivars of heather and the site of the huge cushion-like beds in luxuriant hues rewards visitors who travel to this northern tip of Wisley.

Return through the Pinetum to the Restaurant area via the bridge over the public right of way or via the Riverside Walk

Below: the startling white blossom of *Prunus x verecunda* brings light to the cool and shady Pinetum

Above right: the extensive heather collection transforms Howard's Field into a living carpet of colour

Below: *Araucaria araucana*, the monkey puzzle, brings a hint of the exotic to the Pinetum

DEVELOPMENT & FACILITIES

FUTURE DEVELOPMENTS

As Wisley nears the beginning of its second century the Society has invited a leading landscape designer and an eminent architect to provide a master plan which will give the garden a new unity without any loss of its distinctive character and charm. It will also provide modern facilities to enhance the Society's scientific, educational and advisory programmes. The Society's vision is to create a centre of horticultural excellence at Wisley which will benefit not just RHS members or Wisley visitors but the millions of gardening enthusiasts worldwide.

The new plans for the garden include:
• a new entrance
• a new network of paths to improve access to the garden especially for the disabled
• a walled garden
• a new glasshouse complex sited on the edge of a new lake
• a science and education centre

In the immediate future, visitors will notice improvements to Seven Acres which include enlarging the lake to link it with the pond; improved visitor access across the area with new hard surface paths; the maintenance and improvement of long vistas over the site, and the development of long term structure planting and seasonal displays of the best shrubs/trees, herbaceous plants and bulbs.

THE NATIONAL COLLECTIONS

The National Council for the Conservation of Plants and Gardens (NCCPG) was established in 1978 to conserve Britain's garden plant heritage. Its main aim was to set up collections of specific plant groups known as National Collections. Wisley is the holder of seven National Collections – Rhubarb, *Crocus, Epimedium, Galanthus*, and heathers (*Calluna, Daboecia* and *Erica*). The rhubarb collection may be found on the Portsmouth Field, heathers in Howard's Field while the remainder are planted throughout the Garden.

REFRESHMENTS

The Conservatory Café and Terrace Restaurant are open all year excluding Christmas Day. Situated to the north of the Laboratory next to the Pinetum, the cafe is a licensed self-service restaurant serving hot and cold snacks, drinks and cakes. There are wooden tables and chairs outside the café available for *al fresco* eating on a sunny day.

Right: visitors enjoy a meal in the sunshine outside the Conservatory Cafe

The Terrace Restaurant, next to the Conservatory Café is a licensed restaurant with a varied menu offering three course meals.

An ice cream parlour sandwiched between the restaurant and cafe is open during the summer months. There is also a kiosk selling snacks, drinks and ice creams open seasonally between the Glasshouses and the Fruit Field.

A similar kiosk may be found next to the woodland picnic area by the car parks.

INFORMATION CENTRE AND BOOK/GIFT SHOP

Next to the main entrance to the Garden, the Information Centre and Book/Gift Shop has the finest selection of horticultural books in the world, complemented by carefully selected merchandise including stationery, specialist food, china, glass, crafts, textiles and much more.

PLANT CENTRE

The Plant Centre offers an extremely wide selection of hardy plants including many unusual species and cultivars. Fruit trees, conservatory and house plants, bulbs and seeds may also be purchased. Both Shop and Plant Centre can be reached from the car park or from inside the Garden.

LIBRARY READING ROOM

The reading room offers access to some of the reference books of the Lindley Library. It is located on the ground floor of Aberconway House, near to the Conservatory Café and Terrace Restaurant. The reading room is open every afternoon and all day Sunday from January to November, and also offers a selection of CDRoms and children's books.

FACILITIES FOR THE DISABLED

Disabled visitors are catered for, and improvements are constantly being introduced to make as much of the Garden accessible as possible. Wheelchairs are available free of charge at the entrance, and admission is free for helpers of wheelchair-bound and blind visitors. Obtain a map with a wheelchair-accessible route at the Entrance.

FRUIT AND VEGETABLES

The kiosk in the car park sells fruit and vegetables harvested from the Garden in season.

Far left: in front of the cafe and restaurant the marquee is assembled for the Wisley Flower Show, a popular event every summer

Left: this informative display in the Plant Centre illustrates a range of plants suitable for a sunny border

EDUCATIONAL EVENTS

The RHS Garden Wisley runs an year round programme of events of horticultural interest. These are open to RHS members and non-members and take place at weekends and during the week.

PRACTICAL DEMONSTRATIONS

Attending demonstrations at Wisley provides an opportunity to learn first-hand a range of practical skills from experienced, professional garden and scientific staff who will pass on their expertise and craftsmanship. It is also a chance to discover more about the techniques and methods used at Wisley.

GARDEN WALKS

Conducted by specialist garden staff, garden walks offer an insight into the development taking place in the Garden and highlight some of the special features, plants and trees which are of particular interest.

AMATEUR COURSES

Limited places on specialist botanical painting, garden design and photography courses are available each year. These very popular courses take place over several days and aim to provide a thorough grounding in each subject.

FAMILY FORTNIGHT

During the school summer holidays, Wisley welcomes its annual influx of children who take part in a fortnight of family fun. A wide range of education and garden-based activities are on offer including creepy crawly talks and trails for the children, storytelling sessions, competitions and fun activities and workshops.

PROFESSIONAL COURSES

For the more dedicated horticulturist Wisley offers an excellent opportunity for study and work, through the Wisley Diploma in Practical Horticulture. This course lasts two years, during which successful applicants are employed full-time by the Society.

In addition, a 12-month period of paid work is available as one of five options under One Year Specialist Certificates.

FOR SCHOOLS AND TEACHERS

As schools concentrate on core curriculum and specific themes within subjects, Wisley offers the unique opportunity of in-service training days for practising teachers and fieldwork opportunities for trainee teachers to raise awareness of plants, gardens and gardening.

School visits are increasingly popular and help to foster children's enthusiasm for, and understanding of, growing plants. Programmes across the age range are available.